Ella Dawn Creations

This journal belongs to:

____

Printed in Great Britain
by Amazon

39513809R00069